HOT SPOTS

AND OTHER EXTREME PLACES TO LIVE

WRITTEN BY
SHIRIN YIM BRIDGES

Published by Pearson Education Limited, 80 Strand, London, WC2R 0RL.

www.pearsonschools.co.uk

Text © Pearson Education Limited 2016
Designed by Bigtop Design Ltd

First published in the USA by Pearson Education Inc, 2016
First published in the UK by Pearson Education Ltd, 2016

20 19 18 17 16
10 9 8 7 6 5 4 3 2

British Library Cataloguing in Publication Data
A catalogue record for this book is available from the British Library

ISBN 978 0 435 16449 2

Printed in China by Golden Cup

Acknowledgements
The publisher would like to thank the following for their kind permission to reproduce their photographs:

(Key: b-bottom; c-centre; l-left; r-right; t-top)

Front cover: Isabella Pfenninger / Shutterstock
Back cover: Robert Matton AB / Alamy

Page 3 Shutterstock.com: V. Belov (br); Tatiana Kholina (r); Isabella Pfenninger (tr); Dr. Morley Read (t); dabldy (bl); Aleksandra H. Kossowska (tl) 6-7 Shutterstock: AndreAnita 6 Alamy Images: Outdoor-Archiv. 6-7 Alamy Images: tbkmedia.de (br); National Geographic Image Collection (cl). 7 Shutterstock.com: Tatiana Kholina (b). 8-9 Alamy Images: Robert Matton AB (t); Outdoor-Archiv (b). 9 Alamy Images: Top-Pics TBK (b). 10-11 Shutterstock.com: V. Belov. 10 Alamy Images: ARCTIC IMAGES (b). Shutterstock.com: V. Belov (cr). 11 Alamy Images: tbkmedia.de (b); Anders Ryman (t). 12 Alamy Images: dave stamboulis (c). 12-13 Alamy Images: Robert Harding Picture Library Ltd. 13 Alamy Images: The Africa Image Library (t). 14 Shutterstock. com: Aleksandra H. Kossowska (bl). 14-15 Alamy Images: Robert Harding Picture Library Ltd (b); Ariadne Van Zandbergen (t). 15 Alamy Images: dave stamboulis (br). 16-17 Alamy Images: Ariadne Van Zandbergen. 16 Alamy Images: imageBROKER (b); Ariadne Van Zandbergen (t). 17 Alamy Images: Horizons WWP (cr); Horizons WWP (b). 18-19 Shutterstock.com: Radu Bercan (b); MrGarry (c); Fotomicar (t); pcruciatti (c).

All other images © Pearson Education

Picture Research by: Caitlin Swain

HOT SPOTS

AND OTHER EXTREME PLACES TO LIVE

WRITTEN BY
SHIRIN YIM BRIDGES

CONTENTS

Life on Earth

Most people on Earth live where it never gets very hot or very cold. More than half of all people in the world live in or near cities. More than half of all people in the world live within 160 kilometres of the sea.

Many of Earth's people live in quite similar places. When you watch a TV programme, the places in which the characters live often don't look very different from where you might live.

But if you looked down at Earth from above, you wouldn't see many cities. A lot of Earth is jungle, mountains, deserts or large areas of snow. What would it be like to live in some of these areas?

Let's meet some people living in extreme places.

Roaming the Arctic Circle

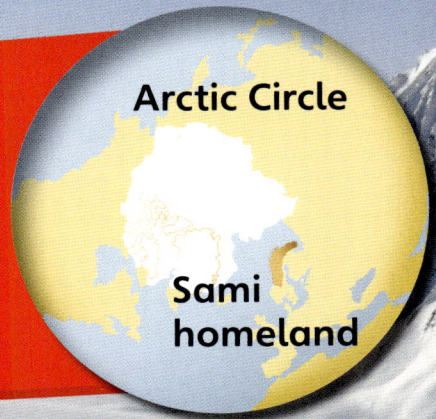

Arctic Circle

Sami homeland

Did you know there are people who use reindeer to pull their sledges? The Sami people do this. In the past, the Sami spent their lives roaming the Arctic. They followed the enormous reindeer herds.

The Sami Homeland

CLAIM TO FAME:
This is the furthest north that human beings live – 322 kilometres north of the Arctic Circle!

AREA:
388 500 square kilometres, about the size of Norway

COUNTRIES:
Sápmi, the Sami name for this area, spreads across what is now northern Norway, Sweden, Finland and Russia's Kola Peninsula.

UNDERNEATH THE MIDNIGHT SUN

The Sami live so far north that in the summer the sun never sets!

Midnight

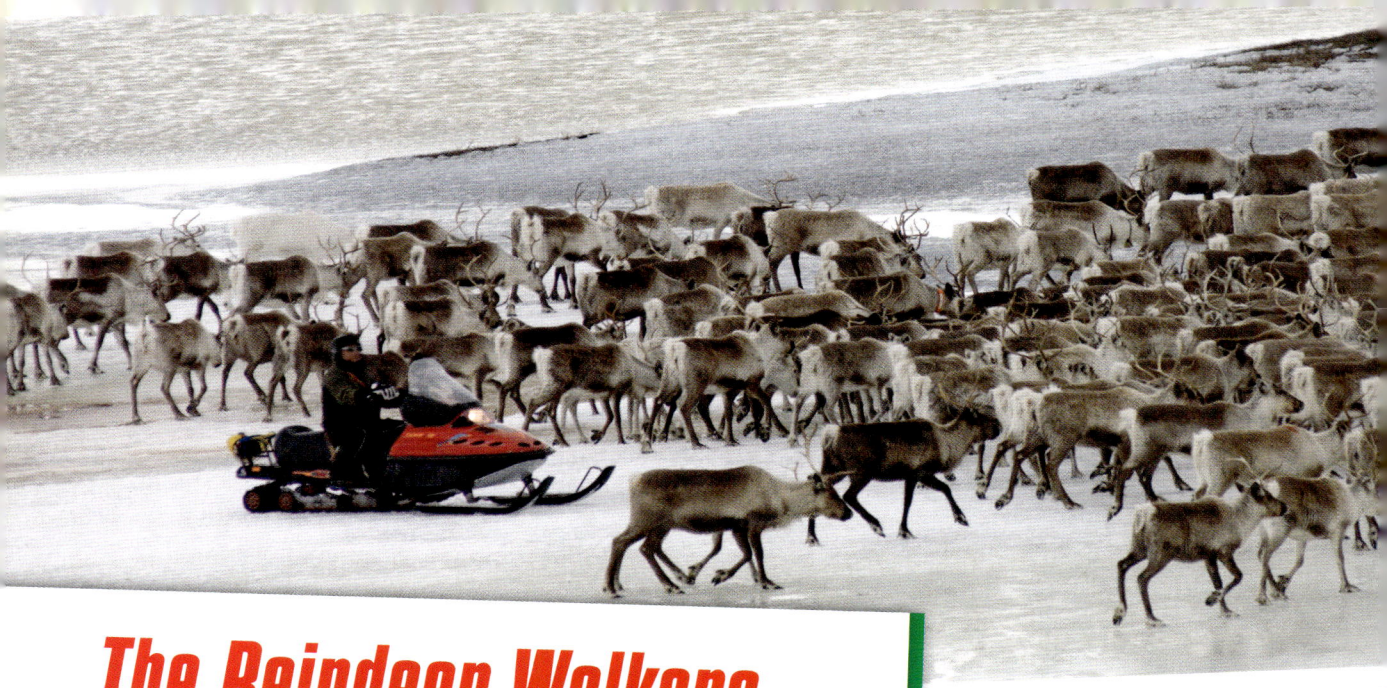

The Reindeer Walkers

The Sami call people who herd
reindeer *boazovázzi*. This means
"reindeer walkers". The herders
used to follow the reindeer by
foot or on skis. They now use
snowmobiles to herd their reindeer.

An All-in-One Animal

Reindeer provide the Sami with
meat, hides and antlers. Most
reindeer are allowed to roam free.
Some are kept for milking and to
pull sledges. Some reindeer can
even be saddled like horses!

The Many Uses of Reindeer

FOOD: Reindeer meatballs, reindeer sausage and smoked reindeer are all very popular.

MILK: Reindeer can be milked like cows.

MEDICINE: Reindeer antlers are sold to China because many Chinese people believe the antlers have **medicinal** properties.

CLOTHING: Reindeer have hairs that are hollow and filled with air. This trapped air makes reindeer fur very warm.

TRANSPORT: Reindeer can be trained to pull sledges; larger **species** can be ridden like horses.

TOOLS: Traditionally, reindeer bones were made into tools such as needles and knives.

Homes on the Go

When moving with their herds, the Sami still live in cone-shaped tents. These are called *lavuts*. A lavut can stand winds that are 80 kilometres an hour. The top of each lavut is open to let out the smoke from large fires.

WHY THE POINTY TOES?

The turned-up, pointy toes of a traditional Sami reindeer-skin boot are designed to hook onto skis.

Clothes with a Code

The lavut is not the only part of traditional Sami life still in use today. The traditional Sami clothing is called the *gakti*. It is still often worn on special occasions. The colours, patterns and buttons of a gakti are a code. They can tell you whether the person is married and which village he or she comes from.

ROUND OR SQUARE BUTTONS?

Traditionally, square buttons mean a person is married. Round buttons mean a person is not married.

Surviving in One of Earth's Hottest Spots

In the middle of the Great Rift Valley in Ethiopia is the Danakil Depression. This region looks like a different planet. It is one of the hottest spots on Earth. It is heated from above by the sun and from below by **lava flows**.

You would think that nobody could live there, but it is home to the Afar. The Afar are **nomadic** people who come to the Danakil Depression every day to mine salt.

NOT A COOL BREEZE

Fire winds blow through the Danakil Depression. They are said to feel like a tornado in an oven!

The Danakil Depression

CLAIM TO FAME:
Daily temperatures of more than 49°C!

ALTITUDE:
91 metres below sea level

RAINFALL:
Less than 18 centimetres a year

CLOSEST CITY:
Mek'ele, 97 kilometres away

Danakil
Depression

Afar Gold

Ten thousand years ago, the Danakil Depression was part of the Red Sea. The waters have evaporated and left behind **salt flats**. To the Afar, this salt is like gold. Until recently, blocks of salt called *amolé* were used as money in Ethiopia. Today, northern Afar people still earn money from selling salt.

Camel Caravans

Every day, Afar miners come to the salt flats with around 2 000 camels and 1 000 donkeys. They transport amolé into the cities. The salt blocks are cut by hand. Everybody in the community takes part. The walk from town to the salt flats and back can take six days.

The Salt Trade

WEIGHT OF ONE SALT BLOCK, OR AMOLÉ:
About 4 kilograms

NUMBER OF BLOCKS PER CAMEL: 30

DISTANCE TRAVELLED PER DAY:
25 kilometres

The Afar live in huts called *aris*.

What Is Life Like in an Ari?

The Afar cross the Danakil Depression to mine salt. They then sell it in the cities. The Afar can do this because they take their homes with them. They pack their houses, called *aris*, onto the backs of their camels. They usually put up their aris around wells. The aris are round, like igloos, and are made from light palm matting. They provide welcome shade in which to cook, eat and sleep.

What's Cooking?

WHAT THE AFAR USUALLY EAT:
Meat

WHAT THEY EAT IT WITH:
Thick wheat pancakes

WHAT THE AFAR DRINK:
Milk

HOW THE AFAR SAY "WELCOME":
They give their guests a drink of milk!

HERDING ANIMALS

In addition to mining salt, most Afar herd sheep, goats, cattle and camels.

What's It Like Where You Live?

Now you've seen some of the extreme places where people live. Can you think of anything extreme about where you live? To an Afar child, where and how you live might look quite different. Many people on this planet have never seen some of the things you probably see every day.

Imagine meeting someone from the Sami or Afar tribe. What would seem extreme to them about your normal life?

Glossary

lava flow   flowing or solid rock that erupted from a volcano

medicinal   having healing properties

nomadic   moving home from place to place

salt flat   area of flat land covered with a layer of salt

species   group of animals or plants that have similar features

Index